From the Library of the
HOMEWOOD PUBLIC SCHOOL
District No. 153

BUILDING A NATION

THE ROAD TO FREEDOM
1750-1783

**Written by:
Stuart Kallen**

THE ROAD TO FREEDOM

Published by Abdo & Daughters, 6535 Cecilia Circle, Edina, Minnesota 55439

Library bound edition distributed by Rockbottom Books, Pentagon Tower, P.O. Box 36036, Minneapolis, Minnesota 55435

Copyright© 1990 by Abdo Consulting Group, Inc., Pentagon Tower, P.O. Box 36036, Minneapolis, Minnesota 55435. International copyrights reserved in all countries. No part of this book may be reproduced in any form without written permission from the publisher. Printed in the United States.

Library of Congress Number: 90-082611   ISBN: 0-939179-88-1

Cover Illustrations by: Marlene Kallen
Inside Photos by: Bettmann Archive

Cover Illustrations by: Marlene Kallen
Edited by: Rosemary Wallner

TABLE OF CONTENTS

Chapter 1: The Growth of Ideas 4
Land of Opportunity
Reading and Writing
Newspapers

Chapter 2: The French and Indian War 8
Conflict in the New World
Trouble in the Valley
The British Win the War
Chief Pontiac War

Chapter 3: Reasons for Revolution 12
New Taxes
The Stamp Act
The Colonists Fight Back
The Results of the Stamp Act
The Move Towards War
The Boston Massacre
Tea Troubles
The British React
The Continental Congress

Chapter 4: The First Battles with the British 23
Lexington and Concord
The Colonies Go to War
American Peace Offer

Chapter 5: The Declaration of Independence 29
July 4, 1776
"Who's Side Are You On?"
The Role of Blacks
Women Patriots
Against All Odds

Chapter 6: The Fight in the North 35
The Conflict in New York
Success in New Jersey
The Failed British Plane
The Hard Winter at Valley Forge

Chapter 7: On to Victory 41
The War in the South
The Patriots Plan for Victory
The Final Blow
The Peace Treaty

Index 47

CHAPTER 1
THE GROWTH OF IDEAS

Land of Opportunity

The *New* World. *New* England. *New* York. Everything about America was new. In 1750, over one million people called the American colonies their home. By 1800, the population had grown to five million.

The oceans teemed with fish. Forests stretched endlessly to the horizon. Farmland was cheap and plentiful. Jobs were available to anyone who wanted them. Life in the New World was full of opportunities.

There was much work to be done and few people to do it. People were needed to build farms, villages and towns. Carpenters, printers, blacksmiths, fishermen and other skilled craftspeople were needed in the cities. Workers were generally well paid for their efforts. People found that if they worked hard, they could improve their lives. Many unskilled people learned trades and crafts. Laborers could earn enough to start their own businesses.

As America grew, it provided people with a better quality of life. Gone were the days when people starved in the wilderness. By the 1750's, towns, villages and cities were growing rapidly all over the thirteen colonies. Life was still hard in the backcountry, but people in the cities found more time for education, ideas and government.

Reading and Writing

The American colonists believed in education. In Europe during the 1700's, only the rich could attend school. One of the ideas taking hold in America was free public education for everyone. As early as 1647, Massachusetts had passed a law requiring towns to build schools. America's first college, Harvard University in Massachusetts was built by the Puritans in 1636. By the 1750's almost every town and village had a public school. All the large cities had universities.

Newspapers

Because more colonists were attending schools, more people were learning to read. Almost all the books, however, were printed in Europe. They were too expensive for most families. Most people could afford only a Bible and one or two other books. For this reason, newspapers became the main reading material for colonial people.

First Harvard Hall, Harvard University.

Newspapers were inexpensive and they reported ideas and events that were happening all around the world.

Besides world events, newspapers reported what was happening in the colonies. Because of their mass circulation, newspapers could educate large numbers of people about important topics. And, American newspapers were doing something exciting and new. They were criticizing the government and its officials. In Europe, nearly all the newspapers were controlled by the government. In America, independent and educated publishers printed whatever they thought was right.

In 1736, the governor of New York arrested the publisher of the *New York Weekly Journal.* Its editor, John Peter Zenger, had accused the governor of being dishonest. Zenger was put on trial but was quickly set free by the jury. The trial showed the English rulers that the colonists had a right to criticize their government. Freedom of the press would become one more revolutionary idea in the thirteen colonies.

CHAPTER 2
THE FRENCH AND INDIAN WAR

Conflict in the New World

England was not the only country that had colonies in America. The French and the Spanish also claimed ownership of huge portions of the New World. The Native American's right to their homeland was ignored.

For centuries in Europe, England, France and Spain had fought wars between themselves. When the New World was discovered, the countries had new reasons to fight. America had a great wealth of natural resources. Each European country wanted to control as much American territory as possible. Farmland, timber, furs and minerals were plentiful. In 1754, the conflict between France and England exploded into warfare in America.

The French respected the Native American's land claims in the New World. The English, however, had been steadily pushing the Native Americans off of the land. When war between England and France broke out in 1754, the Native Americans fought on the side of the French. The conflict became known as the French and Indian War. Because the war lasted seven years, it is sometimes called the Seven Years War.

The French and the Indians fight the British during The French and Indian War.

Trouble in the Valley

The Ohio River snakes through western Pennsylvania and northern Virginia. In the 1750's, thousands of English colonists moved to the lush forests and fertile farmland of the beautiful Ohio River Valley. The rapid increase of English settlements alarmed the French who had land claims there.

The French wanted to protect their landholdings in what they called New France. They built a chain of forts along the St. Lawrence, Mississippi and Ohio rivers. The English colony of Virginia also claimed the Ohio River Valley as its property. The governor of Virginia wanted the French to leave the Ohio Valley. He threatened war if the French did not obey. On October 31, 1753, the governor of Virginia sent George Washington, a twenty-one-year-old soldier, to deliver his message to the French.

Washington hiked for eight days through the dense forests of Virginia. He delivered the governor's message to the French commander. The commander was polite, but refused to leave the Ohio Valley.

In May 1754, Washington led 150 soldiers into western Pennsylvania to construct forts for the British. While Washington's troops were building a fort, the French and their Native American allies attacked them. Washington's soldiers were outnumbered and surrendered to the French. Over the next two years, the French and Native Americans scored many victories over the British.

The British Win the War
In 1762, the Spanish entered the war on the French side. Although the British lost many battles, they won the war in 1763. France surrendered all of its lands east of the Mississippi River. Spain surrendered Florida to England. With the Spanish and French removed from their borders, England became the most powerful country in the world. Soon the English settlers began to push westward.

Chief Pontiac War
The land that the European countries were fighting over rightfully belonged to the Native Americans. The Iroquois and other tribes had been living in the area for thousands of years.

But now the English settlers were moving in. The tribes wanted to regain their lands. Forty Native American tribes banded together under the leadership of Chief Pontiac. The Native Americans fought bravely against the British, but they were no match for the British guns. By the fall of 1764, the Native Americans had been beaten.

After the British had beaten the Native Americans, some of their chiefs met with the British generals to negotiate a peace treaty. England said they would give the Native Americans all of the lands west of the Appalachian Mountains. During the peace talks, the British commander, General Jeffery Amherst, gave the Native Americans blankets that he knew were infected with the smallpox virus. As a result, thousands of Native Americans died in a smallpox epidemic that was started on purpose by the British.

CHAPTER 3
REASONS FOR REVOLUTION

New Taxes

The joy that England felt over its victory in the French and Indian War was short-lived. The war had drained the English treasury. And the size of the English territory had nearly doubled. The English government was forced to spend more money to control the colonies with extra soldiers and administrators. Also, the victory in the war had brought a new sense of unity and confidence to the colonists. They no longer wanted the British supervising their affairs. The time was right for the colonists to declare their independence.

England was losing money on the American colonies. The money that the English spent in America was provided by British taxpayers who were already overtaxed. Most colonists had ignored the taxes that they were supposed to be paying to the British government. England decided that the American colonists should pay the costs of running their colonies.

Parliament, Great Britain's government, decided to pass several new laws for America. One law passed in 1765 was to ease the cost of keeping soldiers in America. The law was called the Quartering Act. It stated that colonists were to provide housing, blankets, candles and food to British soldiers. But the colonists became angry when soldiers started to move into their homes.

The Stamp Act

Despite much protest from the colonists, Parliament passed the Stamp Act of 1765. The law required that colonists buy special stamps to put on a wide variety of items. Newspapers, marriage licenses, calendars, even playing cards and dice, had to have stamps on them. The stamp showed that a tax had been paid on the item. The list of goods to be taxed was six pages long. Violators of the Stamp Act were put on trial before a judge without the benefit of a jury.

Not only did the colonists dislike paying taxes on so many items, but the tax brought up other issues as well. The American colonies had no representatives in the British Parliament. American colonists felt that if laws were passed concerning them, they should be passed by the colonial governments. The phrase "taxation without representation" became the fighting words for the angry colonists.

The Colonists Fight Back

Before the Stamp Act went into effect, furious colonists went into action. Groups of men calling themselves the Sons of Liberty organized secret clubs to fight the act. Women organized the Daughters of Liberty.

From Massachusetts to South Carolina, the Sons and Daughters of Liberty stopped stamped papers from being unloaded from wagons. They protested at tax collectors' homes. They threatened to coat the tax collectors with tar and feathers. In Massachusetts, a mob hanged and burned a stuffed doll that looked like the local tax collector. Then they went on a rampage. They tore down the stamp tax collector's warehouse board by board. Then they went to the tax collector's home and destroyed it.

The Results of the Stamp Act
Other groups protested the Stamp Act in more responsible ways. People wrote letters to England's King George III to protest the tax. People stopped buying British goods at the market. Soon Parliament was forced to repeal the tax.

The British had caused themselves a lot of trouble with the Stamp Act. Never before had the American colonists been so organized against the British government. Even more important, colonial protests against the Stamp Act brought into public view men who would haunt the British government for years to come. John Adams,

Patrick Henry, George Washington and Thomas Jefferson all fought the Stamp Act. Later, these men would be the chief organizers of the American Revolution.

The Move Towards War
The colonists were thrilled over the repeal of the Stamp Act. But the British treasury was still in need of money. The problem was made worse when Britain suffered a depression in 1767. People in England demanded that their taxes be reduced. To raise money, Parliament decided to tax English items sold in America. Glass, tea, silk, paper, paint and lead were all taxed. The colonists were outraged.

In 1768, the American colonists started a boycott of the taxed British items. They refused to buy the taxed items. Before long, colonists were manufacturing the items that they had previously been buying from the British.

The Boston Massacre
The hostilities took a turn for the worse in 1768. That year, England sent two regiments of soldiers to Boston. For a year and a half, the soldiers camped on Boston Common while angry citizens taunted them.

Unrest in the American British colonies between the "Sons of Liberty" and the British soldiers.

On March 5, 1770, a crowd of several hundred colonists gathered in front of the Boston customs house where taxes were collected. Ten soldiers stood guard in front of the customs house. The crowd began to jeer and curse the soldiers. The crowd pelted them with snowballs, icicles, oyster shells and sticks. Suddenly a shot rang out. When the soldiers heard the shot, they opened fire on the crowd with their muskets.

When the smoke cleared, five members of the crowd lay dead in the street. Six people were wounded. The first man to die was a black sailor named Crispus Attucks. He had been an active member of the Sons of Liberty.

Newspapers all over the colonies reported the Boston Massacre. Later that year, the soldiers were brought to trial. Because a member of the crowd had fired the first shot, the soldiers were set free.

Tea Troubles
In 1770, The British repealed the Quartering Act. They stopped taxes on everything except tea. The boycott ended on everything except tea. People drank Dutch tea that was smuggled into the colonies. An uneasy peace returned.

After several years, the British tea growers in India were feeling the burden of the tea boycott. They convinced Parliament to lower the taxes on tea so that people would buy it again. In 1773, Parliament passed the Tea Act. This act lowered tea taxes but did not allow colonial merchants to sell British tea. Colonists would have to buy tea directly from the British.

For the third time in ten years, colonial people took to the streets in protest. The Tea Act became one more sign of unwanted British interference. People began brewing *Liberty Tea* out of their own herbs. They joined anti-tea leagues and signed anti-tea declarations. Unsold tea rotted on the docks. In Boston and other cities, ships carrying tea were not even allowed to tie up to harbor docks.

In December 1773, the Massachusetts governor ordered British tea ships into Boston harbor to unload. He would not allow the protestors to stop him. On the night of December 16, the Sons of Liberty sent fifty men thinly disguised as Native Americans to the Boston dock. There, the men boarded the tea ship and threw 300 chests of British tea into the ocean. The incident became known as the Boston Tea Party.

The Boston Tea Party — Destruction of the tea in Boston Harbor, December 16, 1773.

The British React

After the Boston Tea Party, the British government decided to punish the people of Boston. Parliament ordered warships to Boston to close the harbor. Ships loaded with food and supplies were an important part of Boston's survival. The British blockade of the harbor forced the city business to stop.

Next, the British government imposed military rule on Massachusetts. They made General Thomas Gage the governor. Town meetings, the legislature and courts were not allowed to hold sessions. The Quartering Act was reinstated and 4,000 British soldiers arrived in Boston. Bostonians were forced to house an army that equaled one soldier for every four citizens.

The Continental Congress

The British efforts to control the colonies only made matters worse. By 1774, the colonies were communicating with each other through a series of pamphlets entitled the Committees of Correspondence. These pamphlets circulated through all thirteen colonies. When the Committees of Correspondence reported the

British blockade of Boston Harbor, food and supplies poured in from all over the country. The Committees of Correspondence helped to unite the colonies. In 1774, the Committees of Correspondence called on the colonies to elect representatives for the First Continental Congress.

On September 5, 1774, the First Continental Congress met in Philadelphia. Representatives from all thirteen colonies except Georgia were there. Among those who attended were George Washington, Patrick Henry, John Adams, Benjamin Franklin and Thomas Jefferson. For six weeks, the men discussed how to avoid war with England. Finally the men sent a letter to King George protesting his actions. They asked for a compromise. The men agreed to meet again in spring. Before they could meet again, however, the first shots were fired in the war known as the American Revolution.

CHAPTER 4
THE FIRST BATTLES WITH THE BRITISH

Lexington and Concord

Few colonists wanted a war with the British. But many felt that war was unavoidable. Preparations began for war as farmers and townspeople started training for battle. The men called themselves *minutemen* because they were prepared to fight at a moments notice.

In the spring of 1775, the British learned that the colonists had guns and gunpowder hidden in the town of Concord, Massachusetts. On April 18, General Gage ordered Major John Pitcairn and 1,000 soldiers to seize the weapons. Pitcairn left Boston at night hoping to surprise the minutemen at dawn.

As Pitcairn's army tramped through the night, they were spotted by Paul Revere, a minuteman. Revere rode through the Massachusetts countryside warning everyone that the British were coming.

Pitcairn and his men soon reached Lexington, a town fifteen miles east of Concord. Seventy minutemen were waiting for his soldiers with muskets ready. Someone — no one knows who —fired a shot. Within seconds, eight colonists were dead and ten were wounded. The British army pushed on to Concord.

The arsenal that Pitcairn thought to be in Concord was very small. After destroying a few weapons, Pitcairn ordered his troops back to Boston. When they encountered 300 minutemen along the road, a British soldier fired *the shot heard round the world.* That shot signaled the beginning of the war.

The road to Boston was lined with over 3,000 minutemen hiding behind fences and barns. By the time Pitcairn's army returned to Boston, 73 British soldiers were dead. Over 200 were missing or wounded.

On April 22, the Massachusetts provincial congress voted to raise 13,600 troops to be commanded by Artemas Ward. When the Continental Congress met again on May 10, 1775, it was to discuss plans for war.

The Colonies Go to War

As the Continental Congress met in Philadelphia, battles were taking place between the colonists and the British. British forts were under attack in New York and Canada. Thousands of minutemen from every part of Massachusetts were pouring into Boston. With ragged uniforms and homemade weapons, the colonists were ready to take on the well trained British army. Because of their red uniforms, the colonists called the British soldiers Redcoats.

On June 12, 1775, the British declared that Boston and the surrounding area were under martial law. This meant that the military would run the city. The British set up camp on Bunker Hill, a high point outside of Boston. From the hill, the British command could keep watch over the city.

When the colonists heard of the British plan, they decided to take control of Bunker Hill and nearby Breed Hill before the British arrived. On the morning of June 17, over 1,500 British soldiers attacked the colonists on Bunker Hill.

The colonists were inexperienced and had little ammunition. The American general, Israel Putnam told his men, "Don't fire until you see the whites of their eyes." The hail of lead from the colonists' guns forced the Redcoats back twice.

George Washington taking command of the American Continental Army.

On the third assault, the British took Bunker Hill as the colonists ran low on ammunition. In the battle, 1,000 Redcoats and 400 colonists were killed.

Even though the battle was won by the British, it was a moral victory for the colonists. The colonists had proven that they could hold their own against the British army.

Two weeks after the battle at Bunker Hill, forty-three-year-old George Washington was appointed commander in chief of the American Continental Army.

American Peace Offer
Although the colonists were fighting the British, many colonists still believed that England had the right to rule them. Most colonists would have been happy to end the war if Great Britian repealed the Tea Act, the Quartering Act and other new laws. But after the battles in Massachusetts, King George was in no mood to bargain with the colonists.

On July 8, 1775, the Continental Congress sent King George the Olive Branch Petition. The petition called for an end to the hostilities and a permanent and happy peace with the colonies. It asked the king to repeal the laws that were causing the troubles.

King George responded to the Olive Branch Petition with an act known as the Prohibitive Act. In it, the king and Parliament ordered all trade to the colonies cut off. They ordered the seizure of colonial ships. And they wanted to bring traitors to justice by hanging them. To make matters worse, the king ordered 10,000 Hessian German soldiers to America to fight for the British. The Hessians had a reputation for looting, arson and uncontrolled violence when they fought.

Attack on Bunker Hill and the burning of Charlestown, June 17, 1775.

CHAPTER 5
THE DECLARATION OF INDEPENDENCE

July 4, 1776
On the 4th of July, 1776, fifty-six men signed a document that would change the history of the world. Most of the document was written by Thomas Jefferson.

The Declaration stated that "all men are created equal." It said that all people are guaranteed "life, liberty and the pursuit of happiness." The document also said that if the government is not following these ideas, the people have a right to change it.

The Declaration of Independence also listed the reasons for the American revolt against the British. It declared America to be a new and independent nation. Declaring America independent was important. As a separate country, Americans could now get help from England's enemies. Also, captured American soldiers would be treated as prisoners of war and not traitors who could be hung.

Fifty-six men signed the Declaration of Independence. The document stated that, "All men are created equal." People were guaranteed "life, liberty, and the pursuit of happiness."

In 1776, America still considered slavery legal. In fact, Thomas Jefferson owned hundreds of slaves. Women and blacks were not allowed to vote. Native Americans had no rights at all. Yet the words written in the Declaration of Independence helped lay a foundation of equal rights for *every* person.

"Who's Side Are You On?"
With the signing of the Declaration of Independence, America became a divided country. About 20 percent of the people in America were still loyal to King George and England. These people were called *Loyalists*. Loyalists tended to be wealthy merchants, former government officials or large plantation owners. Benjamin Franklin's son, the Governor of New Jersey, sided with the British, causing his father much anguish. Some Loyalists went back to Britian or moved to Canada. Most remained quietly in America, keeping their opinions to themselves.

Native American tribes such as the Iroquois, Shawnee, Delaware and Cherokee sided with the British. The tribes hoped that the British would drive the colonists out of their homeland.

Many colonists remained neutral in the Revolutionary War. Some were from religious groups such as the Quakers who did not believe in violence. Some thought the colonists would lose the war.

But the majority of Americans were willing to drive the British from American soil. These people were called *Patriots*. The Americans knew the war would be a hard one. But no one knew the war would last six-and-a half years and involve eighty major battles.

The Role Of Blacks

Most blacks, both free and slave, tended to support the Patriots. Black soldiers had fought at Lexington and Concord, Bunker Hill, and in other early battles. But George Washington did not want black soldiers in the army. He worried that blacks would take the idea of freedom too seriously. He feared that they would have their own revolution. When the British offered freedom to any slave who joined the British army, Washington changed his mind. Eventually, over 5,000 blacks fought for the Patriots in the Revolutionary War.

Women Patriots

Women also played an important role in the Revolutionary War. Women were not allowed to fight, but two women, Deborah Sampson and Sally St. Clair, disguised themselves as men and joined the fight. When Sampson was wounded, a surprised doctor discovered her true identity.

Because women could pass unnoticed through British camps, many women became spies for the Patriots. Other women would follow their husbands' regiments. They cooked, laundered, collected medicines, and nursed the wounded. Benjamin Franklin's daughter, Sarah Franklin Bache, organized a Daughters of Liberty chapter. Her group sewed uniforms and handled hospital shipments. Because the men were away from home, many women maintained farms and built guns, cannons and ammunition.

Against All Odds

Besides being a nation whose loyalties were divided, the colonists faced other problems as well. Great Britain was the strongest military power in the world. British soldiers were well disciplined. They had the finest firearms, tents, uniforms, blankets and other necessities of war.

The American soldiers, on the other hand, were unused to following orders. They were in constant need of food, clothing and ammunition. The British navy had 28 warships with over 500 guns. The Continental Army had no warships.

The main advantage the Americans had was the desire to drive the British from their homeland. A British soldier 3,000 miles from home had much less of a desire to fight than a farmer defending his own home.

Americans also fought differently from the British. When the Redcoats went into battle, they lined up in straight rows. They shot their muskets at the enemy across the field. The enemy was supposed to line up in a similar formation. The colonists, however, hid behind rocks, trees and fences. When the Redcoats marched through the dense American forests, they were easy marks for the sharpshooting Continental soldiers.

CHAPTER 6
THE FIGHT IN THE NORTH

The Conflict in New York

In the summer of 1776, over 32,000 Redcoats marched into New York City. General William Howe was in command. Howe was sympathetic to the Americans. He did not want a battle. He thought the sight of so many soldiers would frighten the Americans into surrendering.

George Washington was not about to surrender. Washington had only half as many soldiers. But he chose to take his poorly armed, untrained troops and fight against the largest military force Britain had ever sent across the sea. Although they fought bravely, Washington's army was pushed out of Manhattan. They were forced to retreat to Pennsylvania.

The battle for New York was just one of many defeats that the Continental Army suffered in 1776. Victories were few, but the American Army gained experience and confidence. Washington realized that the British were not the unstoppable war machine that he feared they would be. Washington felt that somehow his army would defeat the British.

General William Howe.

Success in New Jersey

Although Washington felt confident, he had many problems to overcome. His troops were tired of the horrors of war. Thousands of men began to desert the army. Many had signed up to fight for only one year. On January 1, 1777, their enlistments would end and they would return home. Washington needed a bold plan.

On December 25, 1776, only days before his soldiers' enlistments expired, Washington decided to attack the British. Washington crossed the icy Delaware River with 2,400 troops. They marched to Trenton, New Jersey. Because the British custom was to stop fighting in the winter, the Redcoats were unprepared for battle.

On Christmas night, the Continental Army attacked a group of Hessian soldiers in Trenton. The Hessians, tired from their Christmas celebration, surrendered immediately. Washington recrossed the Delaware with 900 German prisoners.

Four days later, Washington decided to attack again. By now his army had grown to 5,000 as many farmers and townspeople joined the Patriots.

In New York, Lord Cornwallis heard about Washington's victory. He decided to march his army to Trenton to wipe out Washington once and for all.

All night long the fires burned brightly in the Patriot's camps. Cornwallis marched toward the fires. When he arrived at dawn, Washington and his soldiers were gone. They had slipped away into the night and taken the town of Princeton, New Jersey. The astonished Cornwallis returned to New York. Washington did not have the troops and supplies to hold Princeton so he spent the winter stationed in nearby Morristown.

The Failed British Plan

In the winter of 1777, the British made plans to divide and conquer the Continental Army. The British would form three separate armies. They planned to take over New York and cut off Massachusetts from the rest of the colonies. If the plan worked, the British would be victorious.

The British battle plans called for one army to fight its way south from Canada along the Hudson River. General John Burgoyne would command this army. Another army led by Colonel Barry St.

Leger would push east through the Mohawk Valley. A third army commanded by General Howe would fight north from New York City. The three armies would meet in Albany, New York. There, they would wipe out the Patriots and cut off New England.

The plan failed miserably. General Howe decided to capture Philadelphia on his way to Albany. Howe succeeded and disrupted the Continental Congress. He also beat Washington at the battle of Brandywine, but his soldiers were unable to join Burgoyne's army.

Burgoyne had troubles of his own. He had a series of successful battles as his army fought through New York. But without help from Howe, he soon faced many defeats. His large army was harassed by the hit-and-run warfare of the Patriots. Although he knew it was a bad idea, he ordered his army to retreat to Saratoga, New York.

Burgoyne's army met 15,000 Patriots at a narrow pass near Saratoga. With the river on one side and steep, dense forests on the other, the Patriots fought the British to a standstill. When Burgoyne, faced with heavy casualties, tried to return to Canada, he found the Patriot army blocking his path. Burgoyne had no choice but to surrender.

On October 17, 1777, over 6,000 Redcoats laid down their guns.

The Battle of Saratoga was a major victory for the Americans. It wiped out the entire British army in the north. News of the victory reached Benjamin Franklin in Paris. He had spent a year trying to convince the French to join the American cause. He was not having much luck. When the French heard about the victory at Saratoga they changed their minds. Soon, France entered the war on the side of the Americans.

Before long, French warships appeared along the coast of America full of supplies. Because of the French commitment, other countries began to join the Americans. Military experts, supplies and money soon started pouring in from Spain, Germany, Poland and the Netherlands.

The Hard Winter at Valley Forge

George Washington had decided to spend the winter of 1777-1778 camped near Valley Forge, Pennsylvania. From a hillside, Washington could keep an eye on the British troops in nearby Philadelphia.

Unfortunately, Washington had made a bad decision. The people that lived in the area were British Loyalists. They refused to sell food and supplies to Washington's battered troops. Local merchants sold Washington bad food and shoddy supplies. Many American soldiers did not even have coats and shoes. As the frigid winter dragged on, the 2,898 soldiers stationed at Valley Forge passed the snowy days with dirty rags wrapped around their bodies and feet. Somehow, Washington kept his army together.

CHAPTER 7
ON TO VICTORY

The War in the South
In 1779, the British generals made one more attempt to permanently crush the American Revolution. The war had already lasted four years. Although the Americans lost more battles than they had won, they were not about to give up. This time the British decided to attack the South.

The new commander of the British Army was the hot tempered Lord Cornwallis. After suffering stinging defeats from Washington, Cornwallis was eager to punish the Americans. Cornwallis chose to attack the South because he thought that many Loyalists lived there. He also thought he could use the British Navy to move troops from place to place. The Americans would have to travel overland.

Once again the British were wrong. There were not as many Loyalists in the South as Cornwallis had thought. Most southerners were strong supporters of the Patriots. They provided the American army with food and supplies. The southerners also acted as spies for the Patriots. They provided the American generals with vital information about trails and shortcuts through the countryside. The French Navy's warships prevented the British from having complete control of the seas.

For awhile, the British plan seemed to be working. The Redcoats captured Savannah, Georgia, in 1778. The American forces tried but could not retake the city. Early in 1780, the British surrounded the most important port in the South, Charles Town, South Carolina. British guns pounded the city until the Americans were forced to surrender. Losing Charles Town was a serious setback for the Patriots.

The Patriot's Plan for Victory

The British had scored some major victories in the South. Many thought the British soon would win the war. But Lord Cornwallis still believed in the traditional European battle tactics. While the Redcoats would line up for the battle, the Patriots would jump from behind trees, shoot, and run.

George Washington sent General Nathanial Greene to command the troops in the South. Greene had a plan that would cost the British the war. Greene's troops would hide in the woods and shoot at the Redcoats. When the Redcoats went after the Patriots, they would disappear into the woods. The Redcoats were pulled further and further into the woods where they became easy targets for the sharpshooters. After several months of this kind of warfare, Cornwallis had lost more than half of his army.

The Final Blow

In 1781, Lord Cornwallis decided to set up fortifications on a sandy peninsula in Yorktown, Virginia. With their backs to the sea, Cornwallis' men dug trenches and built sand walls to fend off an attack from the land. They expected the British Navy to protect them from any attack from the sea.

George Washington had been waiting to attack a major British force from the land and sea at the same time. Cornwallis gave him the opportunity. Washington marched to Yorktown with 5,000 French reinforcements. At the same time, thirty French warships with 3,000 marines sailed up Chesapeake Bay to attack Cornwallis.

Attacked from the land and sea, Cornwallis' army held off the Patriots for three weeks. American muskets punished his troops. The French ships rained down cannonballs. On October 17, 1781, Cornwallis surrendered.

American and French troops lined up facing each other in a column a half a mile long. The British were forced to walk the column as the American band played "And the World Turned Upside Down." The Redcoats walked into an open field where they piled their muskets. Although there were still 16,000 British troops in New York, the war was over. When news of the American victory spread through the colonies, church bells rang and people celebrated in the street.

Cornwallis resigning his sword to Washington.

The Peace Treaty

Benjamin Franklin met with the British and signed a peace treaty. In it, the British recognized America as an independent nation. The treaty was signed November 30, 1782. It was ratified by the American Congress on April 19, 1783, exactly eight years to the day after the first shot was fired at Lexington.

No one was more amazed by the victory than George Washington. He had defeated the greatest war machine on earth with a group of ragtag, underequipped, half-starved men. The Patriots had faced the most horrible conditions that a human could stand. And they did it all for no pay. Their own nation based on freedom, independence and equality were the rewards for which the Patriots fought. Now it was time to forge a new nation.

INDEX

ADAMS, JOHN   15, 22
AMERICAN COLONIES   3, 4, 6
AMERICAN REVOLUTION   16, 22, 32, 33, 41
AMHERST, GENERAL JEFFERY   12, 37, 38
ATTUCKS, CRISPUS   18

BACHE, SARAH FRANKLIN   33
BATTLE OF SARATOGA   39
BOSTON   16, 21, 22, 24, 25
BOSTON MASSACRE   16-18
BOSTON TEA PARTY   19, 20, 21
BREED HILL   25
BUNKER HILL   25, 27, 32
BURGOYNE, GENERAL JOHN   38, 39

CHARLES TOWN, SOUTH CAROLINA   42
COMMITTEES OF CORRESPONDENCE   21, 22
CONCORD, MASSACHUSETTS   23, 24, 32
CONTINENTAL ARMY   26, 27, 34, 35, 36, 37, 38, 39
CONTINENTAL CONGRESS   21, 22, 24, 25, 27, 34, 36
CORNWALLIS, LORD   38, 41, 42, 43, 44, 45

DAUGHTERS OF LIBERTY   14, 15, 33
DECLARATION OF INDEPENDENCE   29, 30, 31
DELAWARE RIVER   37

FRANCE   8, 10, 11, 40, 44
FRANKLIN, BENJAMIN   22, 40, 46
FRENCH AND INDIAN WAR   8-9, 12

GAGE, GENERAL THOMAS   21, 23
GEORGE III, KING OF ENGLAND   15, 22, 27, 28, 31
GREENE, GENERAL NATHANIAL   43

HARVARD UNIVERSITY   5, 6
HENRY, PATRICK   16, 22
HESSIANS   28, 37
HOWE, GENERAL WILLIAM   35, 36, 39

JEFFERSON, THOMAS   16, 22, 29, 31

LEXINGTON   23, 24, 32, 46
LIBERTY TEA   19
LOYALISTS   31, 41, 42

MASSACHUSETTS   5, 15, 21, 23, 24, 25, 27, 38
MINUTEMEN   23, 24, 25
MISSISSIPPI RIVER   10, 11

NATIVE AMERICANS   5, 8, 11, 12, 19, 31
NEW YORK   4, 25, 35, 39

OHIO RIVER   10
OLIVE BRANCH PETITION   27, 28

PARLIAMENT   13, 14, 15, 16, 19, 21, 28
PATRIOTS   32, 33, 37, 39, 42, 43, 44, 46
PHILADELPHIA   22, 25, 39, 40
PITCAIRN, MAJOR JOHN   23, 24
PONTIAC, CHIEF   11, 12
PROHIBITIVE ACT   28
PURITAN   5
PUTNAM, ISRAEL   25, 26

QUAKERS   32
QUARTERING ACT   13, 18, 21, 27

RED COATS   25, 27, 34, 35, 37, 40, 42, 43, 44
REVERE, PAUL   23

ST. CLAIR, SALLY   33
ST. LAWRENCE RIVER   10
ST. LEGER, COLONEL BARRY   38
SAMPSON, DEBORAH   33
SAVANNAH, GEORGIA   42
SLAVERY   31
SMALLPOX   12
SONS OF LIBERTY   14, 15, 18, 19
SPAIN   8, 11, 40
STAMP ACT   14, 15, 16

TAXES   13, 14, 15, 16, 18, 19
TEA ACT   19, 27

VALLEY FORGE, PENNSYLVANIA   40, 41

WARD, ARTEMAS   24
WASHINGTON, GEORGE   10, 11, 16, 22, 26, 27, 32, 35, 37, 38, 39, 40, 41, 43, 44, 45, 46

YORKTOWN, VIRGINIA   43

ZENGER, JOHN PETER   7

DATE DUE